The Dinosaur King

Written by Isabel Thomas

Illustrated by Steve Brown

OXFORD
UNIVERSITY PRESS

OXFORD
UNIVERSITY PRESS

Great Clarendon Street, Oxford, OX2 6DP, United Kingdom

Oxford University Press is a department of the University
of Oxford. It furthers the University's objective of excellence
in research, scholarship, and education by publishing
worldwide. Oxford is a registered trade mark of Oxford
University Press in the UK and in certain other countries

Text © Isabel Thomas 2017
Illustrations © Steve Brown 2017
Inside cover notes written by Karra McFarlane

The moral rights of the author have been asserted

First published 2017

All rights reserved. No part of this publication may
be reproduced, stored in a retrieval system, or transmitted,
in any form or by any means, without the prior permission in
writing of Oxford University Press, or as expressly permitted
by law, by licence or under terms agreed with the appropriate
reprographics rights organization. Enquiries concerning
reproduction outside the scope of the above should be sent to the
Rights Department, Oxford University Press, at the address above.

You must not circulate this work in any other form
and you must impose this same condition on any acquirer

British Library Cataloguing in Publication Data
Data available

ISBN: 978-0-19-841507-7

10 9 8 7 6 5 4 3

Paper used in the production of this book is a natural, recyclable product
made from wood grown in sustainable forests. The manufacturing process
conforms to the environmental regulations of the country of origin.

Printed in China

Acknowledgements
Series Editor: Nikki Gamble

Tops was cracking nuts. She felt a bump on her horn.

"Help!" said Tops. "The sky is falling down!"

"I must tell the Dinosaur King," she said.

Tops set off to see the Dinosaur King.

Tops met Steg.

"The sky is falling down!" said Tops.
"I am off to tell the Dinosaur King."

Tops and Steg met Comp.

"The sky is falling down!" said Tops.
"We are off to tell the Dinosaur King."

"I will come, too," said Comp.

"Come in," said the Dinosaur King. "Sit next to me."

He was planning to munch the little dinosaurs for lunch!

"The sky *was* falling down," said Comp.

"I was right!" said Tops.

"Shall we go back and look for nuts?" said Steg.